THE BEGINNERS BUSINESS GUIDE TO PROFITABLE AMARANTH FARMING

Cultivating Success: A Comprehensive Guide to Profitable Amaranth Farming for Beginners

KARAN IRIS

© 2024 by KARAN IRIS

All rights reserved .Except for brief quotations included in critical reviews and certain other noncommercial uses allowed by copyright law, no part of this book may be reproduced, distributed, or transmitted in any form or by any means, including photocopying, recording, or other electronic or mechanical methods, without the publisher's prior written permission.

DISCLAIMER

This book's content is only meant to be used for general informative purposes. Although the author has taken great care to ensure the content is accurate and thorough, no warranties or assurances on the information's accuracy, correctness, or reliability are provided. It is recommended that readers employ their own judgment and discretion when applying any material found in this book to their particular situation.

The information in this book is not intended to replace professional advice, nor is the author an expert in any of the subjects covered. It is recommended that readers consult with experienced professionals regarding any particular issues or concerns.

Any name that may be mentioned or referred in this book does not imply endorsement, recommendation, or relationship on the part of the author with any person, entity, good, website, or association. These references are made only for informational purposes and are not meant to be taken as recommendations or endorsements.

The information contained in this book may cause readers to suffer loss or damage, for which the author disclaims all obligation and accountability. The only people accountable for the decisions and actions taken by readers using the information presented are themselves.

Any names, characters, companies, locations, activities, occasions, and incidents referenced in this book are either made up or the result of the author's imagination. Any likeness to real people, living or dead, or to real things is entirely coincidental.

This book's content may change at any time, without prior notice, according to the author. The onus is on the reader to verify whether there have been any updates or revisions.

The reader accepts the conditions of this disclaimer by reading this book. Please do not read this book or use its contents if you do not agree to these terms.

Table of Contents

CHAPTER 1 12

   AN OVERVIEW OF FARMING AMARANTH .12

   What is the amaranth herb? 12

   History and Origins of Amaranth Farming 12

   Uses and Advantages of Amarath 13

   What Makes You Desire to Grow Amaranth ... 14

   Amaranth Market Overview 15

CHAPTER 2 18

   COMMENCING AMARANTH FARMING 18

   Selecting the Right Sorts of Amaranth 18

   The Soil and Climate Needs for Amaranth 19

   Tools and Equipment Needed for Farming Amaranth 20

   Designing Your Amaranth Farm's Layout 20

   Legal and Regulatory Considerations for Amaranth Farming 21

CHAPTER 3 24

   PREPARING THE SOIL AND PLANTING 24

   Soil Analysis and Testing 24

Soil Amendments and Fertilization..................25

Selecting and Starting Seeds 26

The Best Ways to Grow Amaranth 27

Irrigation and Water Management 28

CHAPTER 4..30
AMARANTH PLANT UPKEEP AND MAINTENANCE...30

Microbiology and Insect Management in Amaranth Production......................................30

Weed Control Strategies 32

Pruning and Thinning Trends 35

Monitoring Plant Health and Growth 37

Evaluating Amaranth's Readiness for Harvest 39

Harvesting Techniques for Maximum Yield...40

Post-Harvest Handling and Storage................41

Quality Control Measures for Amaranth Products 43

CHAPTER 6..46

FARMERS' MARKETING APPROACHES FOR AMARANTH 46

Identifying Your Perfect Clientele 46

Identifying and Packing Your Amaranth Products 47

Amaranth Item Pricing Pointing Strategies 47

Channels of Distribution for Amaranth Farmers 48

Advertising & Promotional Initiatives 49

CHAPTER 7 52

FINANCIAL PLANNING AND MANAGEMENT 52

Budgeting for the Production of Amaranth: ... 52

Compilation of Profit Margin and Cost Analysis: 54

Financial Risk Management Strategies 56

Bookkeeping and Maintaining Documents: 57

Seeking Funding and Investment Opportunities: 59

CHAPTER 8 62

EXPANDING YOUR FARM BUSINESS USING AMARANTH 62

Evaluating Growth Prospects 62

Increasing Production Capacity 64

Strengthening Your Marketing Campaigns 66

Hiring and Managing Farm Laborers 67

Responsible Approaches for Continued Growth 69

CHAPTER 9 72

ISSUES AND REMEDIES FOR AMARANTH PLANTING 72

Common Challenges Faced by Amaranth Farmers 72

A Guide and Methods for Getting Past Challenges 74

Building Flexibility into Your Amaranth Farming Business 78

CHAPTER 10 82

THE FUTURE PROSPECTS FOR AGRICULTURAL AMARANTH 82

Technological Developments in Amaranth Agriculture 82

Recent Advances in the Market for Amaranth Products 83

Opportunities to Diversify Amaranth Farming 85

Environmental Concerns and Sustainable Practices 86

Future Prospects for Amaranth Farmers 87

CHAPTER 1

AN OVERVIEW OF FARMING AMARANTH

What is the amaranth herb?

Prized for its delectable leaves and grains, amaranth is a versatile and healthy crop. The plant family Amaranthaceae contains several species, such as Amaranthus cruentus, Amaranthus hypochondriacus, and Amaranthus caudatus. Because they are abundant in protein, these plants are a vital supplement to diets worldwide.

History and Origins of Amaranth Farming

Over thousands of years, amaranth has a rich and famous history that began in Mesoamerica and South America. Ancient societies like the Incas and Aztecs prized amaranth as a staple grain due to its high nutritional content and ability to adapt to many temperatures. Nevertheless, during the Spanish invasion, its cultivation declined due to its ties to indigenous religious practices. In recent decades, there has been a global surge in interest in amaranth due to its nutritional profile and sustainability.

Uses and Advantages of Amarath

Amaranth's numerous health advantages make it a valuable crop for both human consumption and animal feed. Because of its high protein content and presence of essential amino acids like lysine, it is a complete protein source that is beneficial for vegetarians and vegans. In addition, amaranth contains no gluten, thus even those with gluten sensitivity can consume it.

There are numerous uses for amaranth. Its grains can be cooked and consumed like quinoa or rice, or they can be popped like popcorn for a crunchy snack or ground into flour for baking. Amaranth leaves are a nutrient-dense green that works well in soups, stir-fries, and salads. They are also known as Chinese spinach or callaloo.

Apart from its culinary uses, amaranth finds its application in traditional medicine due to its purported anti-inflammatory and antioxidant properties. The oil extracted from the seeds is used in cosmetics and as a cooking oil.

What Makes You Desire to Grow Amaranth

There are many advantages for farmers and the environment in growing amaranth. It is first and foremost a resilient crop that can thrive in a range of conditions, from damp to dry. This adaptability reduces the likelihood of crop loss due to outside factors.

Because of its high protein content and nutrient density, amaranth is a financially successful crop in terms of nutrition, especially in regions where malnutrition is prevalent. It also satisfies the growing demand for alternative grains from health-conscious consumers because it is gluten-free.

Furthermore, amaranth is a sustainable crop because it uses less water than other common grains like wheat or corn. Its deep root system improves soil structure and lowers soil erosion, which in turn increases long-term land productivity.

Amaranth Market Overview

The market for amaranth has expanded dramatically in the last several years as more people become aware of its versatility and health benefits. The market encompasses a variety of businesses, including food and beverage, pharmaceuticals, cosmetics, and animal feed.

The food industry's amaranth products, which please health-conscious consumers searching for healthful, gluten-free options, include whole grains, flour, and snacks. The increasing demand for plant-based proteins has led to an expansion of the market for protein powders and supplements made from amaranth.

As an animal husbandry feed ingredient, amaranth is gaining popularity due to its high protein content and amino acid composition. By doing this, you can encourage healthier animals and reduce the need for traditional feed sources.

The pharmaceutical and cosmetic sectors, which use compounds made from amaranth for their purported health and skincare benefits, allow further market expansion and diversification.

All things considered, the amaranth market has a great deal of promise for farmers, food producers, and other stakeholders looking to capitalize on the rising demand for healthful and sustainable agricultural products.

CHAPTER 2

COMMENCING AMARANTH FARMING

Selecting the Right Sorts of Amaranth

A successful farming enterprise depends on choosing the appropriate varieties of amaranth. The following are crucial things to remember:

1. **Intention**: Determine if you are growing for decorative, grain, or leaf purposes.

2. **Climate Suitability**: Select cultivars that are adapted to the local climate.

3. **Growth Habit**: Consider bushy or erect varieties, depending on your farming area and harvesting methods.

4. **Yield Potential**: Look for cultivars with high yields if you want to expand your harvest.

5. **Disease Resistance**: Use resistant cultivars to lower crop losses.

The Soil and Climate Needs for Amaranth

To grow amaranth, one must comprehend the appropriate soil and climate:

1. **Climate**: Amaranth thrives at warm temperatures (25–35°C) and can tolerate dry environments.

2. **Soil Type**: Loamy, well-drained soils with a high organic matter content are the best.

3. **pH Level**: A pH range of 6.0-7.5 is ideal for optimal growth.

4. **Sunlight**: Six to eight hours of sunlight every day are necessary for plants to grow healthily.

Tools and Equipment Needed for Farming Amaranth

The administration of your amaranth farm requires the following machinery and tools:

1. **Soil Preparation**: Prepare the ground with plows, harrows, and cultivators.

2. **Planting**: Use planters or seed drills for even distribution of seeds.

3. **Irrigation**: Drip or sprinkler irrigation systems deliver a consistent flow of water.

4. **Weeding**: Use mechanical weeders or hand instruments like hoes to pull weeds.

5. **Harvesting**: Use motorized harvesters, sickles, or scythes for efficient harvesting.

Designing Your Amaranth Farm's Layout

Optimizing resources and output can be achieved by designing a productive farm layout:

1. **Spacing**: When calculating the spacing between rows and plants, consider the variety and growth method.

2. **Pathways**: Ensure that you have easy access to crops and a convenient path for equipment movement.

3. **Water Source**: Make sure you are near water sources so that irrigation will be easier.

4. **Shade Management**: Consider your options when it comes to shading delicate plants or in bad weather.

5. **Storage**: Allocate room for equipment and storage of harvested produce.

Legal and Regulatory Considerations for Amaranth Farming

Observing legal and regulatory requirements is crucial for farming enterprises to function properly:

1. **Licenses and Permits**: Obtain the licenses and permits needed to use land, use water extraction, and apply pesticides.

2. **Environmental Regulations**: Adhere to regulations concerning waste management, biodiversity protection, and soil preservation.

3. **Crop Insurance**: Consider your options for insurance coverage to protect against crop losses caused by pests or natural disasters.

4. **Labor Laws**: Ensure compliance with regulations on wages, work hours, and farm worker safety.

5. **Market Regulations**: Find out about the guidelines that control the amaranth product market, such as price and quality standards.

It is easier to achieve sustainability and long-term success in amaranth farming if these aspects of your business are taken care of.

CHAPTER 3
PREPARING THE SOIL AND PLANTING

Soil Analysis and Testing

For amaranth farming to be successful, soil analysis is crucial. By providing vital information on pH levels, soil nutrients, and overall health, they assist farmers in making well-informed decisions about managing their land. Here's what you should be aware of:

1. **Importance of Soil Testing**: Deficits in nutrients have a direct effect on plant growth and yield and can be detected by soil testing. It also establishes the soil's pH, texture, and organic matter content—all of which are critical for amaranth growth.

2. **Testing Procedure**: Collect soil samples from different parts of your land at different depths. Send these samples to a reputable soil testing facility so they can be examined. Usually

included in the results are the levels of nutrients (nitrogen, phosphorus, potassium, etc.), pH, and recommendations for amendment.

3. **Reading the Results**: Understand the soil test report. It will suggest specific soil amendments or fertilizers based on nutritional deficiencies. It can be necessary to modify the pH balance or the quantity of organic components.

Soil Amendments and Fertilization

Amaranth plant growth and yield depend on a balanced nutrition supply. To accomplish these objectives, soil amendments and fertilization are necessary:

1. **Organic Amendments**: Improve the soil with mulch, compost, or other organic resources. These amendments improve the soil's structure, water retention, and nutrient availability over time.

2. **Inorganic Fertilizers**: Based on the findings of a soil test, add inorganic fertilizers to the soil to replenish any nutrients that are lacking. Follow recommended application rates to avoid overfertilization, which can harm plants and the environment.

3. **Timing**: Apply fertilizers and nutrients before seeding or according to the crop's growth stages. This ensures that when plants need nutrients the greatest, they will be available.

Selecting and Starting Seeds

For an abundant yield of amaranth, choosing premium seeds and ensuring proper germination is crucial:

1. **Seed Quality**: Select authentic seeds from reputable suppliers. Desirable traits include high germination rates, disease resistance, and soil and climatic adaptation.

2. **Optimal Germination Conditions**: Ensure that the temperature, light, and moisture levels are just correct (about 70–80°F/21–27°C). Consider using seedling trays or a nursery set up for consistent germination.

3. **Seed Treatment**: Treat seeds as necessary to protect them from diseases or pests. Treat seeds according to recommended guidelines to avoid harming germination or the plant's health.

The Best Ways to Grow Amaranth

Using the right planting techniques can have a big impact on amaranth output and development. Follow these suggested guidelines:

1. **Spacing and Depth**: Space amaranth seeds 12 to 18 inches apart and at the recommended depth of 1/4 to 1/2 inch. This promotes ideal growth and discourages crowding.

2. **Soil Moisture**: When planting and throughout the early phases of growth, make sure the soil has adequate moisture. Give the seeds a gentle irrigation once they are sown, and maintain a consistent soil moisture level throughout the growing season.

3. **Weed management**: Use effective weed control methods to lessen competition for nutrients and water. Herbicides may be used to control weeds if organic agriculture practices allow it, or mulching and hand weeding are other methods.

Irrigation and Water Management

To grow and develop healthily, amaranth needs enough water. Techniques for irrigation and water management that work are crucial:

1. **Watering Requirements**: Pay careful attention to the soil's moisture content and water amaranth plants as needed. Aim for a consistent moisture level; avoid damp and dry conditions.

2. **Irrigation approaches**: Depending on the size, type of soil, and availability of water on your farm, choose the appropriate approaches. Options include drip irrigation, furrow irrigation, and sprinklers. Adapt watering regimens to plant growth stages and weather conditions.

3. **Water Conservation**: Use water-saving techniques, including as mulching, soil moisture sensors, and scheduling irrigation for cooler times of the day, to reduce water loss from evaporation.

If you apply these techniques, your amaranth farming enterprise will be well-equipped to produce profitable crops while promoting soil health and sustainability.

CHAPTER 4

AMARANTH PLANT UPKEEP AND MAINTENANCE

Microbiology and Insect Management in Amaranth Production

Growing amaranth has challenges due to pests and illnesses that can compromise output and quality, much like any other agricultural endeavor. Managing pests and pathogens effectively is crucial for the successful cultivation of amaranth. These are crucial points to keep in mind:

1. **Identification:** Regular scouting is required to identify pests and illnesses early on. In addition to leaf spots and powdery mildew, frequent pests

in amaranth farming include caterpillars, flea beetles, and aphids.

2. When applying an Integrated Pest Management (IPM) strategy, chemical, biological, and cultural control methods are combined. Among these strategies include crop rotation, the introduction of beneficial insects, the use of pest-resistant cultivars, and the sparing application of pesticides.

3. **Organic Pest Control:** Physical barriers such as row covers, predatory insects such as ladybugs, and neem oil sprays are some non-chemical methods to deter pests from damaging plants.

4. **Disease Prevention:** The first line of defense against infections is the selection of cultivars resistant to disease. Moreover, keeping

good hygiene habits, such as getting rid of contaminated plant debris, might help stop the spread of illness. Plants must be positioned correctly to provide for enough air circulation.

5. **Monitoring:** Regularly check plants for signs of disease or infestation by insects. Because early detection allows for prompt response, it lessens harm and the need for strict control measures.

Weed Control Strategies

Overall productivity is decreased as a result of weeds and amaranth plants competing for nutrients, water, and sunlight. Successful weed-control methods include the following:

1. **Cultural Practices:** Tilling the soil thoroughly and mulching it are two good strategies to keep weeds from growing on your land. Another way to keep weeds at bay is to plant in dense stands.

2. **Mulching:** By covering your soil with organic materials like straw or grass clippings, you can prevent weed growth and maintain soil moisture. Cotton and plastic mulches are also excellent options.

3. **Mechanical Control:** Cultivators and other mechanical instruments, as well as manual weeding and hoeing, can be used to physically eradicate weeds. Time is crucial in preventing the development and spread of weed seeds.

4. **Herbicides:** Conventional farming can apply selective herbicides according to label guidelines if they are certified for use in amaranth cultivation. It is essential to follow safety procedures and avoid pesticide drift.

5. **Crop Rotation:** By rotating amaranth with crops that have different growth patterns or allelopathic properties, it is possible to disrupt amaranth life cycles and reduce weed pressure.

Timetable for Nutrient Management and Fertilization

Correct nutrition management is essential for amaranth to achieve optimal growth and yield. Consider the following:

1. **Soil Testing:** Check the pH and nutrient levels of the soil before planting. The amount of fertilizer to use can be estimated using this data.

2. **Balanced Fertilization:** Based on the results of a soil test, apply a balanced fertilizer or organic amendments to give essential elements such as potassium, phosphorus, and nitrogen. Adjustments may be necessary throughout the growing season.

3. **Organic Fertilizers:** Compost, manure, and cover crops are examples of organic sources that can provide soil fertility and slow-release nutrients.

4. **Fertilization Schedule:** Divide fertilizer applications into three stages: pre-planting, side-dressing during early growth, and additional supplements as needed depending on plant development and nutrient uptake.

5. **Micronutrients:** Examine your intake of these nutrients and, if necessary, take supplements. Foliar sprays or soil treatments can be used to address micronutrient deficiencies.

Pruning and Thinning Trends

Proper pruning and thinning in amaranth cultivation promotes stronger plants and higher yields:

1. **Thinning:** Plants should be spaced far enough apart to allow for proper growth and nutrient absorption without pushing out neighboring plants.

2. **Pruning:** Remove dead or unhealthy plant sections to prevent diseases from spreading and to improve overall plant vigor. Pruning with caution will encourage branching and more productive development.

3. **Timing:** Thin and trim plants during the early development stages when they are actively growing but not yet strained or overwhelmed.

4. **Tools:** Use clean, sharp pruning shears to make precise cuts without injuring plants.

5. **Training:** Tie or stake plants gently as needed to encourage upright growth when working with tall varieties that are prone to lodging, especially in windy conditions.

Monitoring Plant Health and Growth

Ongoing observation is necessary for the assessment of plant health and prompt problem-solving.

1. **Visual Inspection:** Regularly check plants for signs of illness, insect damage, malnutrition, or environmental stresses such as waterlogging or drought.

2. **Recordkeeping:** Maintain a log of the dates of planting, the applications of fertilizer, any insect or disease observations, and the stages of growth. Monitoring progress and making educated managerial decisions are made easier by this data.

3. **Environmental Monitoring:** Pay attention to factors like temperature, humidity, and rainfall that can affect how plants develop and become vulnerable to pests and diseases.

4. **Integrated Approach:** Integrate data from sensors or monitoring equipment with visual observations to obtain a comprehensive picture of plant health and environmental conditions.

5. **Responsive Action:** Based on monitoring data, take proactive measures to optimize plant growth and health. These could involve changing the way that plants are watered, introducing nutrients or pesticides, or implementing cultural customs.

By using these strategies and keeping a close eye on the health and development of their plants, growers may boost the profitability of their amaranth farming operations.

Section Five

Harvesting and Post-Harvest Management

Naturally, of course! This comprehensive guide covers all the topics related to farming amaranth:

Evaluating Amaranth's Readiness for Harvest

- **Growth Stage Monitoring**: Pay close attention to the stages at which the amaranth plants are growing. They are typically ready for harvesting when they are fully developed yet still delicate.

- **Visual Indicators**: Look for visual cues like as mature seed heads, vibrant leaf color, and firm stems to determine whether something is ready.

Seed Development: Wait until the seed heads turn brown and the seeds become solid enough to rub off before harvesting.

Taste and Texture: Taste and feel the leaves and seeds to ensure they are at their peak nutritional richness and flavor.

Harvesting Techniques for Maximum Yield

Timing: Harvest in the early morning or late afternoon to avoid the plants being stressed by the heat.

- **Cutting Method**: Use sharp tools to cut the plants at the base to harvest the leaves; alternatively, gather the seed heads to harvest the seeds.

- **Staggered Harvest**: Remove mature plants while allowing others to reach a different stage of growth to guarantee a consistent yield.

Gentle Handling: To avoid damage and maintain the quality of the finished product, exercise extreme caution when handling the harvested plants.

- **Efficiency**: Optimize harvesting techniques to maximize yield while minimizing waste and labor costs.

Post-Harvest Handling and Storage

- **Cleaning**: Get rid of any dirt, debris, and damaged areas to prolong the shelf life of harvested amaranth.

- **Drying**: Allow amaranth leaves and seeds to air dry entirely to prevent mold growth and preserve quality.

- **Storage Containers**: Store dried amaranth goods in airtight bags or containers to protect them from moisture and pests.

Cool, Dry Location: Keep amaranth in a cool, dry place away from direct sunlight to maintain freshness.

Monitoring: Watch for any signs of deterioration or insect infestation in the amaranth that has been stored, and act quickly to address any issues that arise.

#4 Preparing the Seeds and Leaves of Amaranth

Seed Extraction: To extract the seeds from the seed heads, use threshing techniques like crushing or rubbing to get rid of the chaff.

- **Cleaning Seeds**: Sieve or winnow the seeds to remove any remaining debris.

Leaf Processing: Give amaranth leaves a thorough wash and sanitization before transforming them into fresh goods or drying them out for storage.

- **Value-Added Products**: If you want to broaden your product offering, think about offering snacks, dietary supplements, or amaranth flour.

Packaging: Processed amaranth products should be packaged in a visually appealing and secure way to maximize marketability and shelf life.

Quality Control Measures for Amaranth Products

Quality Standards: Establish and adhere to standards for amaranth product purity, freshness, and nutritional content.

Testing: Conduct routine testing for moisture content, microbiological activity, and nutritional analysis to ensure product quality and safety.

- **Traceability**: Implement traceability mechanisms to track the movement of amaranth products from farm to consumer to increase accountability and transparency.

Feedback Loop: Get input from stakeholders and consumers to meet market expectations and consistently improve product quality.

- **Compliance**: Keep up-to-date knowledge of licenses and regulations concerning the production of amaranth and the assurance of its quality.

Understanding and applying these tips for harvesting, post-harvest management, processing, and quality control will help you run a more lucrative and long-lasting amaranth farming operation.

CHAPTER 6

FARMERS' MARKETING APPROACHES FOR AMARANTH

Identifying Your Perfect Clientele

Before using any marketing strategies, amaranth producers must ascertain who their target market is. This means getting to know your potential customers' demographics (age, gender, income level, etc.), psychographics (lifestyle, hobbies, values), and specific needs and preferences about your products. This approach can be aided by surveys, market research, and the examination of current consumer data. By identifying your target market, you can adjust your marketing strategies with more success.

Identifying and Packing Your Amaranth Products

Your branding has a big impact on how customers view your amaranth products. Develop a strong brand identity that encapsulates the best aspects, principles, and unique selling points of your farm. This involves creating a memorable logo, choosing packaging that appropriately communicates the product's quality and sustainability (taking eco-friendly packaging options into account), and developing a consistent brand message across all marketing channels. You can attract loyal customers and differentiate yourself from the competition by building a great brand.

Amaranth Item Pricing Pointing Strategies

When determining the optimal price strategy for your amaranth products, it's critical to consider a variety of factors, including perceived value, market demand, competitor pricing, and manufacturing costs. Among the pricing strategies you can pick from are competitive pricing, which sets prices in line with competitors, cost-plus pricing, which adds a markup to production expenses, and value-based pricing, which bases prices on the perceived value to customers. Pricing experiments and client feedback monitoring can help you fine-tune your pricing approach for optimal profitability.

Channels of Distribution for Amaranth Farmers

Making the right distribution channel choices is essential to successfully reaching your target audience. Consider traditional distribution channels like the farmers' markets, supermarkets, and specialty food stores in your area as well as newer ones like online marketplaces, direct-to-consumer sales on your website, and partnerships with food delivery services. Take into account the reach, price, and appropriateness of each channel with your brand concept to determine the best distribution mix for your amaranth products.

Advertising & Promotional Initiatives

Developing effective marketing campaigns and promotions can improve sales, raise brand recognition, and cultivate a loyal consumer base. Before proceeding, ascertain precise marketing objectives (e.g., an X% rise in sales, the launch of a new product line, or market expansion) and select suitable marketing channels (influencer connections, social media, email marketing, etc.). Make advertisements that appeal to your target market, highlight the unique features of your amaranth products, and captivate viewers with story and visual elements. Consider using promotions like discounts, package discounts, or loyalty programs to boost sales and encourage repeat business.

All things considered, strong branding and packaging, strategic pricing, efficient distribution channels, a deep understanding of the target market, and memorable advertising campaigns tailored to the wants and needs of the target audience are all essential components of successful marketing strategies for Amaranth growers. To maintain profitability and competitiveness in the amaranth farming sector, it is imperative to periodically evaluate and modify your strategies in light of customer feedback, market developments, and corporate objectives.

CHAPTER 7

FINANCIAL PLANNING AND MANAGEMENT

Budgeting for the Production of Amaranth:

The process of budgeting for amaranth farming involves allocating funds to various departments within the business. Important things to consider are as follows:

1. **Property and Infrastructure:** Determine the costs related to purchasing or leasing real estate, tilling the soil, establishing irrigation systems, and building infrastructure, such as sheds and greenhouses.

2. **Seeds and Inputs:** Determine the price of high-quality amaranth seeds, fertilizer, pesticides, and other inputs required for crop cultivation.

3. **Labor Costs:** When hiring farm laborers, ascertain the labor costs, including salary, benefits, and training expenses.

4. **Machinery and Equipment: Set aside money for the purchase or rental of tractors, harvesters, and irrigation machinery, among other farm equipment. Include the cost of maintenance and repairs.

5. **Operating Expenses:** Include the cost of transportation, marketing, utilities (water and electricity), and other administrative fees such as permits and licenses.

6. **Contingency Fund:** Set aside a percentage of the money in case of unanticipated expenses or emergencies, such as severe price fluctuations or crop failures.

7. **Seasonal Variations:** Throughout the year, consider changes in revenue and costs related to planting, harvesting, and market demand.

Compilation of Profit Margin and Cost Analysis:

Calculating profit margins and conducting a cost analysis are necessary steps in determining whether amaranth production is profitable. Here's how you approach it:

1. **Cost Analysis:** Enumerate all farming-related expenses, including labor, seeds, and fixed costs (land, equipment). Use accounting methods like activity-based costing to precisely allocate costs.

2. **Revenue Estimation:** Based on the current pricing of the amaranth market and the yield per acre, estimate the potential revenue. Consider factors like demand fluctuations, quality, and sales channels (local markets, wholesalers, exporters).

3. **Gross Profit Margin:** To calculate the gross profit margin, subtract the whole cost of production from the total revenue and divide the remaining amount by the total revenue. This demonstrates how profitable the farm's operations are.

4. **Net Profit Margin:** Take interest costs and overhead (marketing, administrative, etc.) out of gross profit to find net profit. Net profit is divided by total revenue to get the net profit margin, which represents the farm's overall profitability.

Financial Risk Management Strategies

Risk management is essential to the sustainability of amaranth farming. Here are some strategies to reduce potential risks:

1. **Diversification:** Plant a range of amaranth varieties to lessen the likelihood that a crop may be lost to pests, diseases, or bad weather.

2. **Insurance:** Purchase crop insurance to protect yourself from output losses resulting from pestilential crops, natural calamities, or fluctuations in market pricing.

3. **Market research:** Conduct in-depth market research to understand pricing fluctuations, competing strategies, and demand trends.

Diversify your techniques of selling to reduce your dependence on a single market.

4. **Financial Planning:** Maintain liquid assets and enough cash on hand to meet unforeseen expenses and market swings. Have a fallback plan in place for managing financial crises.

5. **Risk Assessment:** Adjust risk management strategies as necessary to account for evolving market conditions, technological advancements, and changes to legislation that affect the agriculture sector.

Bookkeeping and Maintaining Documents:

Effective record-keeping and bookkeeping practices are crucial for financial management in amaranth cultivation.

1. **Money Records:** Maintain detailed records of all earnings, expenses, loans, investments, and taxes related to farming amaranth.

2. **Crop Monitoring:** Keep accurate records of crop yields, input usage, pest management strategies, and soil management practices. Use digital tools or farm management software for efficient data tracking.

3. **Budget Tracking:** Compare anticipated and actual revenue and expense figures to make the required modifications to financial plans.

4. **Tax Compliance:** Keep meticulous records for tax purposes, including depreciation, credits, and deductions linked to farming. Seek counsel from tax experts to ensure compliance with tax laws and regulations.

5. **Long-Term Analysis:** Using historical financial data, identify trends, evaluate performance, and make educated decisions about impending investments and operational improvements.

Seeking Funding and Investment Opportunities:

Financing and investment alternatives might provide capital for expanding amaranth farming businesses. Consider the following options:

1. **Grants and Subsidies:** Research government funding sources for the implementation of innovative technology, the growth of sustainable farming practices, and market expansion.

2. **Credits and Loans:** Discuss credit lines or loans intended for working capital needs, equipment acquisitions, or farm growth with banks, financial institutions, or agricultural lenders.

3. **Investor Partnerships:** Make an effort to form partnerships with cooperatives, investors, or venture capitalists involved in agriculture ventures. Provide a compelling business plan that highlights anticipated earnings, risk mitigation strategies, and expansion opportunities.

4. **Crowdsourcing:** Utilize platforms that facilitate crowdsourcing to secure funds from individual investors, local advocates, or agribusiness enthusiasts willing to support innovative farming ventures.

5. **Value-Added Products:** Consider diversifying your revenue streams by using amaranth to make flour, snacks, and nutritional supplements, among other value-added products. To attract lenders or investors, highlight the profitability and market demand of the products.

By implementing these financial planning and management strategies, aspiring amaranth farmers can overcome challenges, optimize resource allocation, and achieve sustainable profitability in the agricultural industry.

CHAPTER 8

EXPANDING YOUR FARM BUSINESS USING AMARANTH

Evaluating Growth Prospects

Accurately assessing the risks involved in expanding your amaranth farming business is essential. Begin by conducting a comprehensive analysis of the market's financial viability, rivalry, and demand. Think about items such as:

1. **Market Demand:** Examine customer preferences, industry developments, and demand estimates for products derived from amaranth. Identify potential development opportunities and market niches.

2. **Competition Analysis:** Identify the benefits, drawbacks, market share, and strategies for pricing that your competitors employ. To attract customers, distinguish your items from those of your competitors.

3. **Financial Feasibility:** Consider projected income, investment requirements, and return on investment (ROI) while assessing the expansion's possible financial implications. Perform a cost-benefit analysis to determine profitability.

4. **Operational Capacity:** Evaluate your current operational capacities, accounting for land availability, production efficiency, and infrastructure. Assess if expansion can be funded with existing resources or if more cash is needed.

5. **Regulatory and Environmental Considerations:** Understand the regulations

that control environmental sustainability, certifications, permits, and land usage. Sustain legal compliance to encourage long-term development.

Increasing Production Capacity

To increase the output capacity of your amaranth farming business, take the following actions:

1. **Optimizing Land Use:** Manage soil, rotate crops, and use proper irrigation systems to increase land production. Enhance yield per acre by employing efficient farming techniques.

2. **Investing in Equipment:** Modernize farming machines and equipment to boost output and simplify operations. Consider using automated planting, harvesting, and processing techniques to reduce labor costs and time.

3. **Using Technology:** Utilize technological tools such as agricultural monitoring systems, data analytics, and precision farming to optimize resource utilization, minimize waste, and enhance crop quality.

4. **Scaling Inputs:** Increase inputs like as seeds, fertilizer, and pesticides based on soil nutrient analysis and agronomic guidance. Make sure that the application methods and timing are appropriate for the desired results.

5. **Crop Diversification:** Seek to expand your crop portfolio by growing complementary crops or by adding value-added amaranth-derived products like flour, oil, or snacks. This might lower risk and broaden the market.

Strengthening Your Marketing Campaigns

To effectively expand your marketing campaigns, take note of:

1. **Market Segmentation:** Look at the psychographics, demographics, and behavior of the target client categories to identify which ones to target. Ensure that the messaging and marketing platforms you use are suitable for each target audience.

2. **Branding and Positioning:** Develop a strong brand identity that aligns with your values, USP, and standards of excellence. Showcase your amaranth goods as upscale, sustainable, and health-conscious.

3. **Digital Marketing:** Use digital channels like social media, e-commerce platforms, email marketing, and content marketing to reach a wider audience, engage customers, and boost sales.

4. **Collaborations and Partnerships:** Form strategic partnerships with distributors, eateries, food manufacturers, and retailers to expand distribution channels and penetrate new markets.

5. **Input and Engagement from Customers:** Talk with customers face-to-face as well as via questionnaires, reviews, and other channels. Make greater use of data to improve product offerings, loyalty programs, and customer service.

Hiring and Managing Farm Laborers

When choosing and managing agricultural laborers:

1. **Skills Assessment:** Identify the specific skills and knowledge required for each role, including farm laborers, agronomists, machinery operators, and administrative staff.

2. **Recruiting:** When conducting recruiting, make use of a range of resources, including job boards, agricultural schools, local networks, and recommendations. Assess candidates for training, experience, and cultural fit.

3. **Training and Development:** Provide employees with comprehensive training programs that equip them with the knowledge, abilities, and best practices they require. Encourage professional growth and lifelong learning.

4. **Performance Management:** Clearly state the goals, expectations, and key performance indicators for every employee. Regularly assess performance, provide constructive feedback, and recognize achievements.

5. **Team Building:** Encourage a positive work environment through coordinated efforts, effective communication, and morale-boosting events. Motivate team members to support and collaborate.

Responsible Approaches for Continued Growth

Implementing sustainable practices is critical to the long-term development of amaranth farming:

1. **Soil Health:** Use soil conservation strategies like crop rotation, cover crops, and low

tillage to preserve the fertility, structure, and biodiversity of your soil.

2. **Water Management:** By installing efficient irrigation systems, rainwater collection systems, and water-saving techniques, you can lower water consumption and strengthen your resistance to drought.

3. **Crop Diversity: To enhance biodiversity, cultivate a range of crops, make use of agroforestry, and save native plant species. This improves ecosystem resilience while reducing the strain caused by illnesses and pests.

4. Utilize Integrated Pest Management (IPM) strategies like as crop rotation, biological controls, and resistant varieties to manage pests and diseases while lowering your reliance on chemical pesticides.

5. **Resource Efficiency:** Utilize renewable energy sources, recycle organic waste, and apply efficient farming techniques to make the most out of the available resources. reduce the carbon footprint and environmental impact.

A profitable and ecologically responsible amaranth farming business can be established by evaluating prospects for growth, increasing production capacity, stepping up marketing campaigns, hiring and managing farm laborers effectively, and using sustainable practices.

CHAPTER 9

ISSUES AND REMEDIES FOR AMARANTH PLANTING

Common Challenges Faced by Amaranth Farmers

Amaranth farming has numerous challenges, despite its great potential. The following are some common challenges that amaranth farmers may face:

1. **Pest and Disease Management:** A few pests and diseases that can harm amaranth are leaf miners, aphids, powdery mildew, and damping-off. Yields could be significantly decreased if these are not appropriately managed.

2. **Maintenance of Soil Health:** Constant amaranth farming may cause soil depletion if

proper soil health management techniques, such as crop rotation and the addition of organic matter, are not used.

3. **Water Management:** Amaranth requires an adequate amount of water to reach its maximum potential. Places with few irrigation resources or irregular rainfall may find it challenging to manage water effectively.

4. **Market Volatility**: Changes in supply and demand can cause issues for growers of amaranth, affecting their capacity to turn a profit and obtain access to markets.

5. **Labor Availability:** During the busiest seasons of the year, it might be difficult to locate skilled laborers for tasks like planting, weeding, and harvesting.

A Guide and Methods for Getting Past Challenges

To solve the above-mentioned difficulties, proactive strategies and best practices must be combined:

1. **Integrated Pest Management (IPM):** Use IPM strategies, such as crop rotation, the use of resistant varieties, biological control agents, and sparing pesticide treatment, to manage pest and disease pressure sustainably.

2. **Soil Conservation and Improvement:** Apply conservation agriculture practices, such as low tillage, cover crops, and mulching, to enhance soil health, retain more water, and reduce erosion.

3. **Water-Efficient Farming Strategies:** Use drip irrigation, rainwater collection, and efficient water scheduling techniques to optimize water consumption and lower the likelihood of water scarcity.

4. **Market Diversification:** Examine a range of market channels, such as local markets, restaurants, online marketplaces, and the food processing industries, to reduce dependence on a single market and guard against price fluctuations.

5. **Mechanization and Training:** Invest in appropriate farm equipment and provide farm personnel with the necessary training to boost productivity, reduce dependency on labor, and enhance operational efficiency.

Modification in Response to Changing Market Conditions

Growers of amaranth need to do the following to thrive in a market that is always shifting:

1. **Be Informed:** Keep abreast of legislation developments, market trends, and consumer preferences that could have an impact on the amaranth industry.

2. **Value Addition:** Consider value addition opportunities such as converting amaranth into flour, snacks, or health goods to boost profitability and create a variety of products.

3. **Market Intelligence:** Through market research, customer interaction, and the use of digital marketing technology, identify niche markets, understand client needs, and personalize products.

4. **Collaboration:** Obtain knowledge about the market, enhance product quality, and increase the

product's market penetration by collaborating with retailers, processors, and input suppliers, among other value chain actors.

Controlling Environmental and Climate Factors

Climate change and environmental unpredictability may have an impact on amaranth growth. Among the strategies to address these problems are:

1. **Climate-Resilient Varieties:** Select and cultivate amaranth varieties that withstand local pests, heat, and drought.

2. **Crop Diversification:** To diversify your farm, plant amaranth with other crops that will

boost its growth requirements and offer resilience to climate risk.

3. **Adaptive Farming Practices:** Make use of agroecological methods such as agroforestry, intercropping, and rainwater collection to boost resilience, preserve biodiversity, and reduce the hazards brought on by climate change.

4. **Weather Monitoring:** Use early warning systems and weather forecasting technologies to anticipate extreme weather events and take preventative measures to protect crops.

Building Flexibility into Your Amaranth Farming Business

Consider the following strategies to make your amaranth-developing business more resilient:

1. **Financial Planning:** Establish a strong financial strategy that incorporates cost analysis, budgeting, and risk management strategies to withstand market fluctuations and unforeseen challenges.

2. **Diversified Income Streams:** Take into account additional income streams like agritourism, value-added products, or eco-friendly certifications to diversify revenue streams and reduce dependence on crop sales alone.

3. **Knowledge and Skills Enhancement**: Regularly hone your technical competency, business acumen, and grasp of agronomy through workshops, training, and networking with industry leaders.

4. **Insurance and Risk Mitigation:** Consider risk-sharing arrangements, disaster preparedness

plans, and crop insurance to reduce monetary losses caused by unfavorable events such as crop failures or market downturns.

5. **Community Engagement:** Form partnerships with local communities, agribusiness organizations, and universities to pool resources, pool knowledge, and work together to address issues that affect amaranth farmers.

Aspiring amaranth growers can overcome challenges and establish a profitable and sustainable farming business by utilizing a holistic approach that integrates agronomic innovation, market research, climate adaptation, and business resilience approaches.

CHAPTER 10

THE FUTURE PROSPECTS FOR AGRICULTURAL AMARANTH

Technological Developments in Amaranth Agriculture

Thanks to contemporary technology, amaranth farming is undergoing a transformation that is also enhancing yields and efficiency. Among the noteworthy inventions are:

1. **Precision farming** involves using drones and satellite imagery, monitoring crop health, and making the most use of water and fertilizer.

2. **Biotechnology**: genetically modifying amaranth cultivars to improve their nutritional

profiles and boost their resistance to pests and illnesses.

3. **Vertical Farming**: Using hydroponic systems and vertical buildings to maximize space and resource efficiency while growing amaranth in urban settings.

4. **Smart Irrigation Systems**: These systems automate irrigation to save water by utilizing soil moisture sensors and meteorological data.

5. **Mechanization**: Using state-of-the-art machinery, such as threshers, harvesters, and seeders, to expedite the planting, harvesting, and processing operations.

Recent Advances in the Market for Amaranth Products

Amaranth products are growing in popularity because of their high nutritional value and variety. Key market trends include:

1. **Health and Wellness Boom**: Due to its high protein, fiber, and vitamin content, amaranth is becoming more and more popular as a superfood, attracting customers who are worried about their health.

2. **Vegan Food Movement**: As a staple of plant-based diets, amaranth is gaining popularity as a gluten-free and vegan-friendly food.

3. **Functional Food Applications**: Amaranth is being used in a range of food items, such as pasta, cereals, snacks, and drinks, which is helping to diversify the market.

4. **International Growth**: Farmers and processors are finding greater opportunities to export their commodities as a result of the growing demand for amaranth products overseas.

Opportunities to Diversify Amaranth Farming

Agricultural diversification with amaranth provides several opportunities to lower risk and increase income:

1. **Value-Added Products**: Amaranth's processing into flour, flakes, puffs, and oil increases market share and profitability for the food industry.

2. **Organic and Specialty Variants**: Growing organic and heritage varieties of amaranth cater to specialized markets and command premium pricing.

3. **Amaranth By-Products**: Utilizing leftover amaranth to create compost, fodder for animals, or biofuel boosts the crop's worthwhile reducing waste.

4. **Partnership with Food Companies**: Working together on product development and

branding with food producers can open up new market channels and raise brand awareness.

Environmental Concerns and Sustainable Practices

Sustainable practices can be used to improve the sustainability of amaranth farming.

1. **Agroecological Farming**: Enhancing soil fertility and reducing reliance on synthetic inputs are achieved by crop rotation, agroforestry, and intercropping with nitrogen-fixing plants.

2. **Water Management**: Use drip irrigation, rainwater collection, and water recycling to cut down on water use and protect freshwater supplies.

3. **Biodiversity Conservation**: Plant hedgerows, make use of native pollinators, and protect natural habitats to boost biodiversity and ecosystem resilience.

4. **Reduction of Carbon Footprint**: Greenhouse gas emissions can be decreased by using low-carbon farming practices, such as cover crops and little tillage.

Future Prospects for Amaranth Farmers

Amaranth farmers have a promising future because of several favorable factors:

1. **Increasing Demand**: Consumer awareness of amaranth's nutritional benefits and environmentally friendly farming practices is propelling the market for amaranth products.

2. **Market Expansion**: Emerging markets in Asia, Africa, and Latin America offer significant development opportunities for amaranth cultivation and trade.

3. **Technological Developments**: As farming technology and biotechnology advance,

productivity and profitability will rise even further.

4. **Climate Resilience**: Because amaranth can adapt to a variety of climatic situations, it is a crop that can withstand the effects of climate change.

5. **Policy promote**: Government initiatives that support small-scale farmers and sustainable agriculture can help to support amaranth cultivation.

Novice amaranth growers can build profitable and successful enterprises by utilizing these trends and opportunities in the always-shifting agricultural world.

www.ingramcontent.com/pod-product-compliance
Lightning Source LLC
Chambersburg PA
CBHW071838210526
45479CB00001B/196